A Crabtree Branches Book

eXtreme SPORTS

Snowboarding

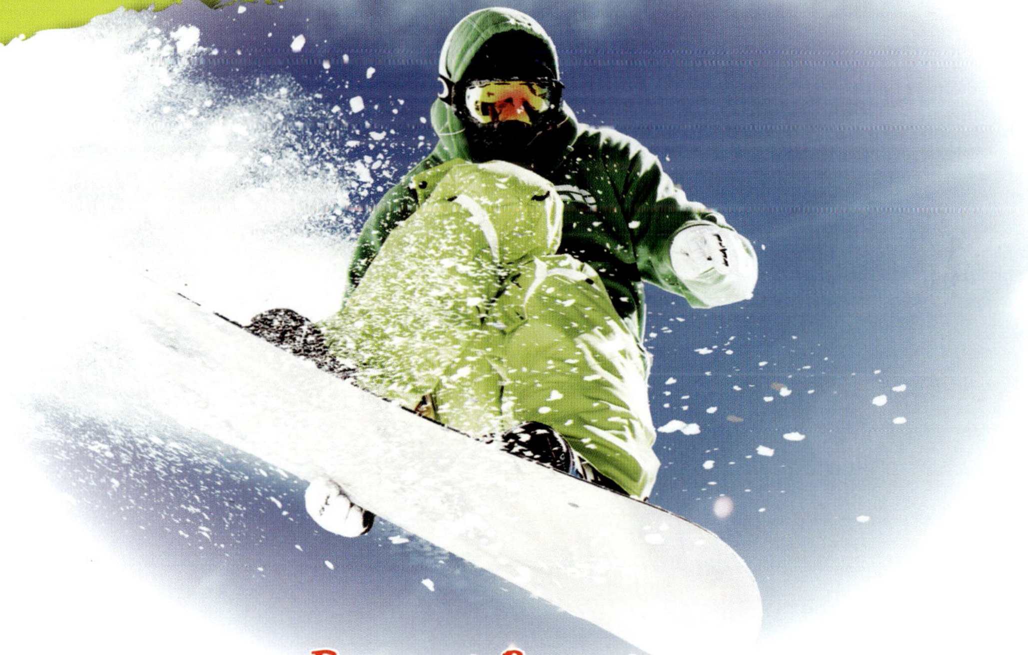

Bernard Conaghan

Crabtree Publishing
crabtreebooks.com

School-to-Home Support for Caregivers and Teachers

This high-interest book is designed to motivate striving students with engaging topics while building fluency, vocabulary, and an interest in reading. Here are a few questions and activities to help the reader build upon his or her comprehension skills.

Before Reading:

- *What do I think this book is about?*
- *What do I know about this topic?*
- *What do I want to learn about this topic?*
- *Why am I reading this book?*

During Reading:

- *I wonder why...*
- *I'm curious to know...*
- *How is this like something I already know?*
- *What have I learned so far?*

After Reading:

- *What was the author trying to teach me?*
- *What are some details?*
- *How did the photographs and captions help me understand more?*
- *Read the book again and look for the vocabulary words.*
- *What questions do I still have?*

Extension Activities:

- *What was your favorite part of the book? Write a paragraph on it.*
- *Draw a picture of your favorite thing you learned from the book.*

Table of Contents

What Is Snowboarding?

Snowboarding is an **extreme** sport. Snowboarders ride down a snow-covered **slope** while standing on a board attached to their feet. They often do different tricks. The first snowboard was invented in 1965 by Sherman Poppen in Muskegon, Michigan. He made it by attaching two skis together and tying a rope at one end for steering.

Fun Fact

Poppen's first snowboard was called a snurfer, a combination of the words snow and surf.

Snowboarding in Action

Snowboarding is one of the most popular extreme sports in the world. There are many types of snowboarding styles. Freeriding is where boarders ride, **carve**, and do jumps on any kind of **terrain** for fun.

Freestyle snowboarding is the most entertaining and thrilling type of snowboarding because of all the tricks that the snowboarders do.

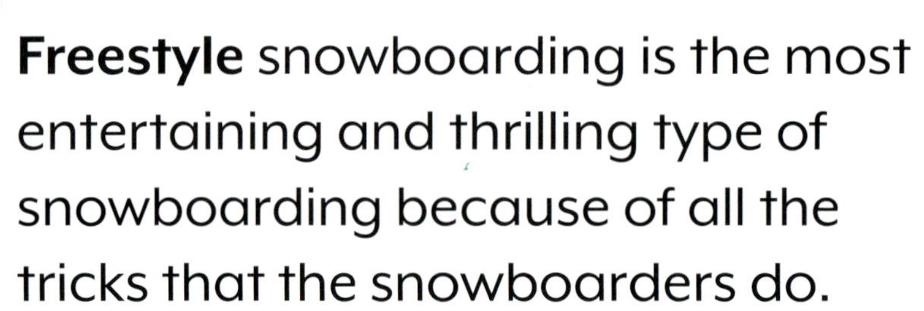

Fun Fact

The U.S. has the most Olympic snowboarding medals.

In freestyle, boarders ride up on a **half-pipe** and do tricks in midair. They also slide down on **rails**.

Freecarve or alpine snowboarding is a type of racing. It is usually done on hard-packed snow. Concentration is important to avoid obstacles such as poles or gates. Freecarve is also an Olympic sport. The snowboards used are longer, narrower, and stiffer.

Fun Fact

There are 11 different snowboarding events in the Winter Olympics.

Jibbing is a style of tricks done in snowboarding. Instead of using **ramp**s, snowboarders jump, slide, and ride on unusual surfaces. These can include metal rails, boxes, benches, ledges, and walls.

In big air snowboarding competitions, snowboarders jump off ramps. They then do flips and other tricks as they soar through the air. Snowboarders are judged on the height they reach in the air, the distance they travel, and the difficulty of their tricks.

Fun Fact

The record number of flips in a single jump is four.

In slopestyle competitions, the boarder does tricks while going down a course. There are obstacles on the course such as boxes, rails, and jumps. The snowboarder who finishes the course with the fewest mistakes and most tricks usually wins.

Parts of a Snowboard

The bottom of the board is called the base. It helps you glide along on the snow. Most bases are made of a material called polyethylene. It has tiny **pores** that soak up wax when heated, and close over when cold. Wax is used on the bottom of the board to increase the speed down the hill.

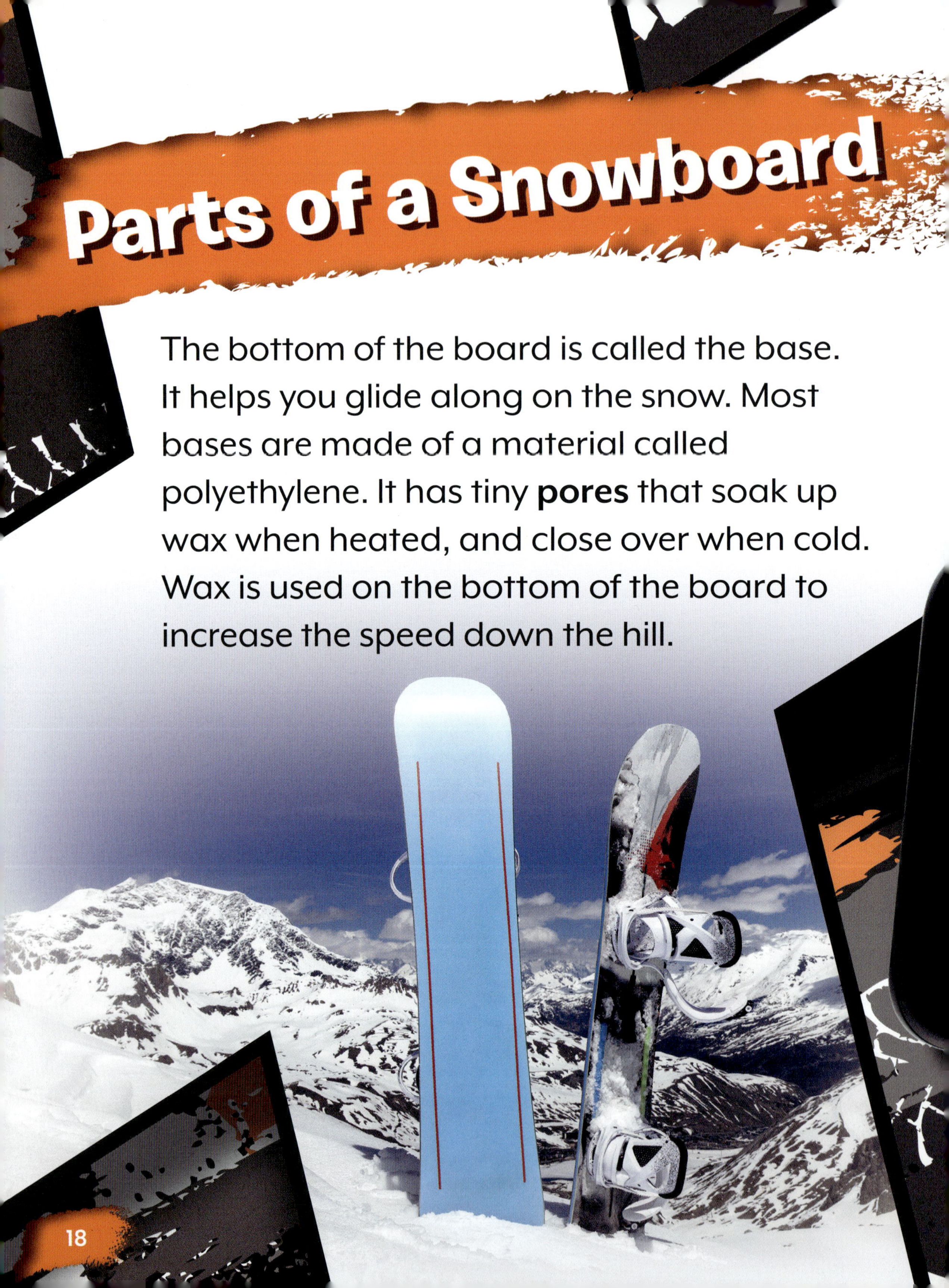

The bindings attach the snowboarder's feet to the board. Baseplates hold the bindings to the board.

Fun Fact

The longest snowboarding jump is 187 feet (57 m).

The topsheet is the outer layer of the snowboard. It is the part that has all the exciting graphics.

Your Snowboarding Career

The best way to start competing in snowboarding is to go to ski hills and practice. Getting a coach to instruct you on the basics of snowboarding can also be helpful. A coach can help train you to compete in snowboarding events.

Fun Fact

Sports in the X Games include snowboarding, skiing, skateboarding, and motocross.

If you become a good snowboarder, you might be able to compete in the Winter X Games or other **tournaments**. The X Games is an extreme sports event held twice a year, in the winter and the summer.

Snowboarding Legends

Throughout the history of snowboarding there have been many different **legends**. One of them is Shaun White. He is a five-time Olympian and a three-time Olympic gold medalist. He was born on September 3, 1986, in San Diego, California.

Another snowboarding legend was Karine Ruby. She won six gold medals and four silver medals at the FIS Snowboard World Championships. She also won a gold medal and a silver medal at the Winter Olympics. Ruby died in a mountain climbing accident in 2009.

Fun Fact

With 67 wins, Ruby holds the record for most Snowboarding World Cup victories.

Glossary

carve (KHARVE): When a snowboarder turns using only the edge of their board

extreme (ek·STREEM): Something that is far beyond the normal

freestyle (FREE·stile): In sports, a performance or competition in which participants are allowed to use different styles or methods

half-pipe (HAF pipe): A curved structure with high sides that is used for doing tricks in snowboarding

legend (LEH·jind): Someone who is famous and admired for doing something well

pore (POHR): A very small opening on the surface of something

rails (RAYLZ): Metal bars that snowboarders use to do tricks

ramp (RAMP): A piece of equipment with a slope

slope (SLOHP): Ground that slants downward or upward

terrain (ter·AYN): An area of land

tournament (TUR·nuh·ment): A competition with many participants

Index

Websites to Visit

www.xgames.com

https://olympics.com/en/sports/snowboard/

www.thesnowpros.org

About the Author

Bernard Conaghan lives in South Carolina with his German shepherd named Duke. Every year he goes snowboarding in Switzerland. He is a coach on his son's football team. He always eats one scoop of peach ice cream after dinner.

Written by: Bernard Conaghan
Designed by: Jen Bowers
Series Development: James Earley
Proofreader: Melissa Boyce
Educational Consultant: Marie Lemke M.Ed.

Photographs: Cover image ©2011 IM_photo/Shutterstock, background ©Matisson_ART/Shutterstock; p.3 ©2020 fotosparrow/Shutterstock; p.4 ©2011 IM_photo/Shutterstock; p.5 phone©2017 Vasin Lee/Shutterstock, ©2007 steba/Shutterstock; p.6 ©2015 Merkushev Vasiliy/Shutterstock; p.7 ©2014 guruXOX/Shutterstock; p.8 ©2018 Leonard Zhukovsky/Shutterstock, medals ©Net Vector/Shutterstock; p.9 ©2010 NatalieJean/Shutterstock; p.11 ©2018 masik0553/Shutterstock; p.12 ©2009 anderm/Shutterstock; p.15 ©2011 Jeff Smith - Perspectives/Shutterstock; p.16 ©2021 Szabo Attila/Shutterstock, ©2019 Lilkin/Shutterstock; p.18 ©2013 Maxim Blinkov/Shutterstock; p.19 ©2017 Dmytro Vietrov/Shutterstock; p.20 ©2011 Yganko/Shutterstock, ©2018 Dragana Gordic/Shutterstock; p.21 ©2013 Graphic Compressor/Shutterstock; p.22 ©2020 fotosparrow/Shutterstock; p.23 ©2017 Dmytro Vietrov/Shutterstock; p.24 ©2019 oliverdelahaye/Shutterstock; p.26 ©2018 Leonard Zhukovsky/Shutterstock, p.27 ©2010 Haslam Photography/Shutterstock, ©2018 Leonard Zhukovsky/Shutterstock; p.28 ©2018 Joaquin Ossorio Castillo/Shutterstock; p.29 https://olympics.com/en/athletes/karine-ruby, ©2016 LiliumBosniacum/Shutterstock

Crabtree Publishing

crabtreebooks.com   800-387-7650

Copyright © 2023 Crabtree Publishing

All rights reserved. No part of this publication may be reproduced, stored in a retrieval system or be transmitted in any form or by any means, electronic, mechanical, photocopying, recording, or otherwise, without the prior written permission of Crabtree Publishing.

Printed in the U.S.A./012023/CG20220815

Published in Canada
Crabtree Publishing
616 Welland Avenue
St. Catharines, Ontario
L2M 5V6

Published in the United States
Crabtree Publishing
347 Fifth Avenue
Suite 1402-145
New York, New York 10016

Library and Archives Canada Cataloguing in Publication
Available at Library and Archives Canada

Library of Congress Cataloging-in-Publication Data
Available at the Library of Congress

Hardcover: 978-1-0396-9665-5
Paperback: 978-1-0396-9772-0
Ebook (pdf): 978-1-0396-9986-1
Epub: 978-1-0396-9879-6